TOD BOLSINGER

TEMPERED RESILIENCE

STUDY GUIDE

8 SESSIONS ON BECOMING AN ADAPTIVE LEADER

An imprint of InterVarsity Press
Downers Grove, Illinois

InterVarsity Press
P.O. Box 1400, Downers Grove, IL 60515-1426
ivpress.com
email@ivpress.com

InterVarsity Press® is the book-publishing division of InterVarsity Christian Fellowship/USA®, a movement of students and faculty active on campus at hundreds of universities, colleges, and schools of nursing in the United States of America, and a member movement of the International Fellowship of Evangelical Students. For information about local and regional activities, visit intervarsity.org.

Scripture quotations, unless otherwise noted, are from the New Revised Standard Version Bible, copyright © 1989 National Council of the Churches of Christ in the United States of America. Used by permission. All rights reserved worldwide.

While any stories in this book are true, some names and identifying information may have been changed to protect the privacy of individuals.

Cover design and image composite: David Fassett
Interior design: Daniel van Loon
Images: burst of glowing lines: © Baac3nes / Moment Collection / Getty Images
  bonfire sparks: © Malorny / Moment Collection / Getty Images

ISBN 978-0-8308-4170-7 (print)
ISBN 978-0-8308-4171-4 (digital)

Printed in the United States of America ♾

InterVarsity Press is committed to ecological stewardship and to the conservation of natural resources in all our operations. This book was printed using sustainably sourced paper.

Library of Congress Cataloging-in-Publication Data
A catalog record for this book is available from the Library of Congress.

P	25	24	23	22	21	20	19	18	17	16	15	14	13	12	11	10	9	8	7	6	5	4	3	2	1
Y	41	40	39	38	37	36	35	34	33	32	31	30	29	28	27	26	25	24	23	22	21	20			

CONTENTS

INTRODUCTION

We will be able to hew out of the mountain of despair a stone of hope.

MARTIN LUTHER KING JR.

MANY OF MY FAVORITE PASTIMES required a guidebook of sorts to get me started. Because I was well into adulthood before YouTube and Google became the go-to source for how-to information, I have a love for guidebooks and cookbooks, for recipes and maps. If I was planning an adventure, I would get the latest Lonely Planet guidebook and the most up-to-date maps. My kitchen is filled with dog-eared cookbooks. But the rise of the digital just-in-time resources means that my smartphone has access to more maps and information than Neal Armstrong had at his disposal when he soared to the moon, or more recipes than Julia Child could translate in a lifetime. So what then of study guides like this?

My previous book, *Canoeing the Mountains*, was published, originally, without a study guide, and we added one later after people started requesting one. People who had the material in the book wanted more tools for processing the lessons and for conversation. Indeed, one of the most interesting things I heard was how many people were using these materials in groups or pairs or teams. Something about learning new material, developing new skills, and talking about what we are learning with people is enlivening, empowering, even inspiring. So, with *Tempered Resilience: How Leaders Are Formed in the Crucible of Change*, we are offering this study guide written specifically with leaders and their partners in mind.

Let me review, however, two assumptions at the heart of everything I write.

First, leadership is a skill that can be taught. Some, of course, have more natural skills or have had life experiences that lead to more quickly understanding the concepts or making the connections to what needs to be learned, but everyone can become a better leader. That shouldn't be a surprise to anyone who knows that I am a seminary professor. We teach students other skills like writing, listening, counseling, interpreting, and preaching. Of course the same caveats about natural abilities apply, but we teach everyone who is admitted to the school. That doesn't mean it is easy. In the book I tell the story of trying to become a better fly-fisher even though I have years of experience in the sport. It was, as I wrote, "a humbling day." Indeed, all learning is hard. Learning skills that do not come naturally to most of us (like staying calm when confronted, asking good questions, and honest self-reflection to the point of deep vulnerability) is even harder. But the book offers a formation process that can be learned by anyone who has the humility and tenacity (two key concepts in the book) to learn, and this study guide seeks to make that process more accessible by breaking down the concepts and the exercises into definable steps.

Second, we learn best in relationships. It shouldn't be a surprise that we learn best with others. I'm a Christian, and the word for learner is *disciple,* and discipleship has always been—right back to Jesus himself—a deeply relational process. *New York Times* columnist and author David Brooks says that we "learn from people we love."[1] And as we discuss in the book, leadership leads to vulnerability that requires the security of relationships to endure. Leading in the face of resistance leaves us feeling exposed, unsure, and often discouraged, so tolerating and learning from the experience of vulnerability is only possible if we know that we are well held by our relationships. The book and this study guide are meant to be shared. They are meant to be read and discussed in relationships. I have structured the sessions in this guide to lead to honest conversations for self-discovery and to offer practices that leaders and their teams can take on together. For an online course covering content related to this book, go to formation.fuller.edu/courses/resilience.

And these two assumptions are even more critical to the subject matter of the particular book this study guide was written for. *Tempered Resilience: How Leaders Are Formed in the Crucible of Change* is about forming leaders to take on the challenge of leading in a changing world. Specifically, it is for the particular purpose of forming resilience in leaders so they can lead through the resistance that always accompanies leading change.

So those two assumptions are at the heart of this study guide: *the formation of leaders who demonstrate resilience in the face of resistance is something that can be learned and requires relationships.*

One final word about this study guide. It mirrors the formation process of the book itself, a process that I illustrate with the way that raw steel is forged into a tool that can be used to hew through and transform the rock-like resistance of people into what Dr. Martin Luther King Jr. called stones of hope. In this book, we discover that

> Tempering a leader is a process of *reflection, relationships, and practices during the act of leading that form resilience to continue leading when the resistance is highest.* It includes vulnerable self-reflection, the safety of relationships and specific spiritual practices and leadership skills in a rhythm of both work and rest. (*Tempered Resilience*, 5)

And so this study guide is broken into sessions that follow the process for becoming a resilient, tempered leader, a process illustrated with the metaphor of blacksmithing:

BECOMING A TEMPERED LEADER

Working: Leaders are formed in leading.

Heating: Strength is forged in self-reflection.

Holding: Vulnerable leadership requires relational security.

Hammering: Stress makes a leader.

Hewing: Resilience takes practice.

Tempering: Resilience comes through a rhythm of leading and not leading.

I should also warn you. This book will be demanding (like Zach, my fishing guide, was with me in a story I tell in the book), but it will hopefully be inspiring (the way so many of the leaders I interviewed were to me). These sessions are formatted in four section that correspond to each step in the tempering process: Review, Reflect, Relate, Practice. The following is an overview of each section before we get started.

REVIEW

In the review section we look back at some of the key concepts. I selected some passages and encourage you to linger over them after reading one or more chapters. You may find that other passages are even more relevant to you during this moment of your leadership. If so, feel free to take up the questions of that section about those passages. But throughout this study guide I'll highlight the main concepts for becoming a resilient, tempered leader.

REFLECT

While there is an entire chapter dedicated to understanding the necessity of vulnerable self-reflection to the formation of a leader, every chapter will take you through specific questions to enable you to reflect on that particular chapter, the insights that need to be learned and the specific challenges for you in your leadership. Included in the "Reflect" section will be the "Consider" questions from *Tempered Resilience* that were written as prompts for self-reflection even as you read through the book.

The "Reflect" section of each lesson can be done either individually or as part of a group discussion. While there will be some specific questions for each section, the basic format of this section is to take the reader to a deeper self-understanding of their leadership practice and the underlying beliefs that result in those leadership practices. So, in every section I offer some new, specific questions and also return to a few of the same questions over and over. These questions are patterned after those that are often used by Ignatian spiritual directors and the process of the prayer of examen that we learn in chapter four.

- What has inspired as you read this chapter of *Tempered Resilience*?
- What raises questions that you would like to have clarified?
- What do you find yourself resisting?
- What changes are you considering in your own leadership because of reading this section?

I highly recommend the use of a journal to capture any insights or to aid in self-reflection using these (and other) prompts throughout the book and study guide.

RELATE

While there is one specific chapter about relationships as the anvil that securely holds the leader during a vulnerable self-reflection process, the "Relate" section of each lesson is written so that teams or groups of leaders can process each chapter together. Think of it as the anvil section for each concept.

In this section some of the questions are meant for leaders to ask each other; others are for the leader to ask others about themselves. Some of these questions you might take to your coach, mentor, or trusted adviser. Others you may ask of your team members or colleagues. Still others are meant to give you a discussion starter with family members or friends.

The goal for the "Relate" section is to build your capacity to find the security you need to be as honest with yourself as possible. This doesn't mean that every question will lead to affirmation and praise but to the confidence that comes through accurate feedback and candid conversations. The internal posture you will need is to be open to feedback, to allow your trusted confidants and team members to speak frankly, and to take personal responsibility for your own growth as a leader.

PRACTICE

Since the goal of *Tempered Resilience* is to help you develop a rule of life for forming you to be resilient in the face of resistance, each lesson focuses on some spiritual and leadership practices for you to incorporate into your life. Remember, leadership is a skill. And skills take practice. So as you take on both spiritual practices to form you and leadership practices to put your formation to work amid your specific leadership context, you'll become the resilient leader that you desire and your people need you to be.

My prayer is that as you read *Tempered Resilience*, work through this study guide, and let the process of *reflection, relationships*, and *practices* (in a *rhythm of leading and not leading*) forge you, you will grow stronger and more flexible, becoming both tempered and resilient. Then you will become even more the leader God has called you to be and that your people need you to be.

1

HEWING HOPE AND THE MOUNTAIN OF DESPAIR

The question I find myself asking is not "Can I learn the skills I need to lead change?" but rather "Can I survive it?"

SENIOR PASTOR OF A LARGE CHURCH

READ the introduction, chapter 1, and chapter 2 of *Tempered Resilience.*

Note: This is the only session that requires more than one chapter of reading. Because so many concepts are set up in these early chapters, this first session is more of an overview of the need for leadership resilience before taking a deeper dive into the metaphor of becoming a tempered, resilient leader.

REVIEW

In *Tempered Resilience* we meet leaders who allow themselves in unguarded moments to talk candidly about the experience of leading change in a rapidly changing world. It is daunting, they admit, and often discouraging. But what takes an even greater toll on leaders than the external challenges they are facing is the *internal* organizational and personal resistance that comes whenever they are trying to bring change within an organization. That resistance can lead to what Edwin Friedman has called a "failure of nerve" as well as what I refer to as a "failure of heart."

> Failure of nerve is caving to the pressure of the anxiety of the group to return to the status quo. . . . Failure of heart . . . is when the leader's discouragement leads them to psychologically abandon their people and the charge they have been given." [1] (*Tempered Resilience*, 28)

Using the ancient biblical story of Moses leading the people of God through the wilderness and the more contemporary story of Dr. Martin Luther King Jr. leading the civil rights movement in the 1960s, *Tempered Resilience* speaks bluntly about the challenges that leaders face when bringing change.

> Leadership . . . is always about the transformation and growth of a people—starting with the leader—to develop the resilience and adaptive capacity to wisely cut through resistance and accomplish the mission of the group. It requires learning and results in loss. And even when we know what we are signing up for, we resist both the vulnerability of learning and the pain of loss. So, to lead, especially in the face of resistance requires that we develop *resilience*.
>
> Resilience is not about becoming smarter or tougher; it's about becoming stronger and more flexible. It's about becoming *tempered*. (*Tempered Resilience,* 4)

Perhaps no challenge is as taxing as when the leader faces sabotage, that is, the resistance from the very people and often the very teammates one has. (See *Tempered Resilience*, 22, for

GROUNDED

A tempered leader can be resilient and withstand both failure of nerve and failure of heart. Both are failures of identity. Succumbing to a failure of nerve means that our sense of identity cannot take the rejection of the people we have been called to lead, so we join them in their anxiety and enjoy their ongoing acceptance. Experiencing a failure of heart means that we become so discouraged, so brittle and cynical, that we disconnect from the people we are called to lead and abandon—either emotionally or physically—both the people and our calling. Failure of nerve in a leader is an identity that becomes enmeshed with followers and loses something of the independence of thought and conviction; failure of heart is evidenced by a leader who becomes disconnected from followers and gives up the call to care and lead the people they have been given.

TEACHABLE   ATTUNED   ADAPTIVE   TENACIOUS   RESILIENT

G R O U N D E D

Figure 1.1

To overcome both failures and stay connected to and faithful to the call to lead a people through change requires Christian identity that is *grounded in something other than one's success as a leader.* (*Tempered Resilience*, 39)

the beginning of a specific example that is woven throughout the narrative of the book.)

Resilience in the face of sabotage is the antidote to the leaders' failure of nerve *and* failure of heart. A tempered, resilient leader doesn't comply with the group anxiety to return to the status quo. And a tempered leader does not become brittle and angry or discouraged and disconnected. Resilience is not something that can be mustered in a moment of "rising to the occasion."[2] It is formed over a long period *before* the crisis of testing so that it can continue the transformation *during* the moment of challenge. Like a soft piece of metal that must be transformed into a chisel to hew a hard granite slab, it has to be worked. The steel has to be transformed—forged and formed and *tempered*—so that it becomes strong and flexible enough to, as Dr. King said, hew stones of hope out of a mountain of despair. (*Tempered Resilience,* 29-30)

REFLECT

General Reflection Questions

1. What has inspired you as you read these chapters of *Tempered Resilience*?

2. What raises questions that you would like to have clarified?

3. What do you find yourself resisting?

4. What changes are you considering in your own leadership because of reading these chapters?

Further Questions for Self-Reflection

- What kinds of challenges have you faced when trying to lead change? Which of those energize you even though they are demanding?

- What kinds of challenges are draining or discouraging to you?

- What is the difference between those kinds of challenges?

- When in your leadership have you suffered from either a failure of nerve or a failure of heart? To which are you more susceptible and why?

- What do you think God is doing in your life that requires you to take on this leadership challenge?

RELATE

Discuss the following with a trusted confidant or group:

- What is one insight from the reading and reflection exercises that would be helpful to process with a trusted confidant or group?
- Share about a time when you experienced sabotage? What toll did it take on you? How did you respond to it?
- In what ways have you experienced leadership challenges as challenges to your identity?
- What happens to you spiritually or emotionally when you experience the resistance of your own team, congregation, or organizational colleagues?

PRACTICE: GROUNDING IN GOD
WHEN FACING RESISTANCE

Using either a journal or in a conversation with a trusted friend, consider this question: What do you need from God for your identity to be grounded in Christ and not in your success as a leader?

Read Matthew 3:1-17 in your favorite Bible version. Slowly and prayerfully repeat verse 17, putting your name in for "my Son." *A voice from heaven said, "This is _____, the Beloved, with whom I am well pleased."*

Now, go back to the original question:

What do you need from God to believe this verse about you?

What difference does believing that make in your leadership?

2

WORKING
LEADERS ARE FORMED IN LEADING

*I've gone through a lot of soul-searching and
agonizing moments. And I've come to see that we have many
more difficulties ahead and some of the old optimism was a little
superficial and now it must be tempered with a solid realism.*

DR. MARTIN LUTHER KING JR.

READ chapter three of *Tempered Resilience.*

BECOMING A TEMPERED LEADER

Working: Leaders are formed in leading.

Heating: Strength is forged in self-reflection.

Holding: Vulnerable Leadership requires relational security.

Hammering: Stress makes a leader.

Hewing: Resilience takes practice.

Tempering: Resilience comes through a rhythm of leading and not leading.

REVIEW

In this chapter of *Tempered Resilience,* we are introduced to my experience of taking a blacksmithing class to learn how steel is turned into something beautiful and useful. Throughout the book we return to the shop and the lessons learned; the first is fundamental to how leaders are developed for the challenges of leadership. In the same way that blacksmiths can only learn from entering the shop, grabbing the tools, feeling the heat of the forge reflecting on their faces, and engaging the task with mind and body, *leaders are formed only while leading.* We can learn *about* leadership by taking classes and listening to compelling lectures or reading books, but actual leadership formation requires entering into the crucible of leadership and facing the challenges—and the resistance—that comes.

In this chapter we learn that the characteristics of a tempered, resilient leader formed in the process of leading are shaped by a grounded identity and by becoming *teachable, attuned, adaptable,* and *tenacious,* that is,

- the *humility to learn* as we go,
- the *capacity to listen* to those who are going with us,
- the *creativity to face challenges with experimentation*, and
- the *persistence to face resistance or rejection.*

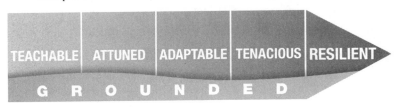

Figure 2.1

REFLECT

General Reflection Questions

1. What has inspired you as you read this chapter of *Tempered Resilience*?

2. What raises questions that you would like to have clarified?

3. What do you find yourself resisting?

4. What changes are you considering in your own leadership because of reading this chapter?

FORGED IN THE FURNACE

Leaders, like tempered tools, are only shaped in the shop. They are only forged in the furnace. They are only made in a place like this filled with both serious work and potential danger. And just as we can't learn to blacksmith or be forged like steel from reading a book or from sitting on a bench, you can't learn to lead without entering into the actual place where the work gets done.

This leads us to the first of two critical introductory points: *Leaders are formed in leading.*

There are books we can read, courses we can take, lessons we can learn through lectures and conversations. But the tempered, resilient leader is forged only in the *process of leading that adds stress to the raw material of our lives.* Which is why it is so difficult and feels so dangerous. . . .

This is not a new insight. Most observers of great and transformative leaders have always known that leadership skill is developed not in the classroom or from the secure area of one's everyday tasks but embedded in a context and embodied in practice amid the challenges of leadership and adversities of life. "It is not in the still calm of life, or the repose of a pacific station, that great characters are formed," Abigail Adams wrote to her son John Quincy Adams amid the American Revolution. "The habits of a vigorous mind are formed in contending with difficulties. Great necessities call out great virtues."[1] . . .

The forming of a resilient leader that occurs amid the very demands of leadership is an ongoing, intense, repetitive, and humbling process of personal transformation.

Whether it is Dr. Martin Luther King Jr. trying to hold together a coalition of civil rights organizations on one side and contend with the vitriol of racist structures and attitudes that have oppressed his people for four hundred years on the other, a nonprofit leader trying to keep offering vital services when government funding has run out, or a pastor leading a congregation to care more for their neighbors than their own preferences while the church is hemorrhaging members:

- Leaders are formed in leading.
- Leadership formation is a hard and humbling, repetitive process of personal transformation. (*Tempered Resilience,* 50-54)

Further Questions for Self-Reflection

Reflect a bit more on this quote from *Tempered Resilience*:

As soon as we have a strong sense of who we are and what we are about, the very demands of leadership challenge us to be open to where we are wrong and where we must be able to grow as leaders to consider that we may be missing the deeper emotional processes that are at work. (*Tempered Resilience,* 58)

- Think of a humble leader you have known or served with. How did this person's humility impact you?
- Review the story about my cultural humility coach (pp. 58-61). Is there an area in your life where you could use some particular coaching through a leadership challenge?

- Which of the attributes of a tempered leader (p. 37) are areas of strengths for you and which are areas that could use further strengthening in order to develop the resilience to lead through change?

RELATE

- With a trusted confidant or group, talk through the attributes of a tempered leader: teachable, attuned, adaptable, and tenacious (see p. 37).

- Ask the confidant or group to give *you* feedback on the same question you reflected on earlier: Which of the attributes of a tempered leader are areas of strength for you and which are areas that could use further strengthening in order to develop the resilience to lead through change?

- Compare their feedback with your self-reflection and discuss any insights, points of disorientation, and potential action steps for strengthening those characteristics.

PRACTICE

Pick one of the following behaviors to focus on as a way of strengthening your leadership resilience: cultural humility, tactical empathy, a compelling why, or biblical perseverance.

What is one change you can make in your daily routine to attend to one of these areas?

What will you need to give up *or* stop doing *to make time for this change?*

3

HEATING

STRENGTH IS FORGED
IN SELF-REFLECTION

*I want to experience your vulnerability but I don't want
to be vulnerable. Vulnerability is courage
in you and inadequacy in me.*

BRENÉ BROWN

READ chapter four of *Tempered Resilience.*

BECOMING A TEMPERED LEADER

Working: Leaders are formed in leading.

Heating: Strength is forged in self-reflection.

Holding: Vulnerable leadership requires relational security.

Hammering: Stress makes a leader.

Hewing: Resilience takes practice.

Tempering: Resilience comes through a rhythm of leading and not leading.

REVIEW

In this chapter of *Tempered Resilience,* we find the fundamental paradox of resilient leadership: strength comes from vulnerability. Indeed, we could say that without experiencing and expressing vulnerability a leader will never be able to cultivate the strength needed to face resistance.

In this chapter we learn that steel has to be heated to almost 2,000 degrees in order to be shaped into a tool. At 700 degrees or so, the tool is dangerously hot ("It can burn the skin off your hands," the blacksmith instructor said), but it looks exactly the same on the outside. At 2,000 degrees, however, the steel has turned from black and gray to orange, yellow, or red; it takes on a molten or "oozy" characteristic that is half-solid, half-liquid, and radiates the heat it is experiencing.

It is tempting to be a leader who stays at 700 degrees, where we experience the heat of conflict, hard decisions, internal resistance, and external challenges but try to never let it genuinely affect us or ever let it show. A 700-degree leader appears fine and in control, but is unable to take in the transformation that could be occurring in their life by experiencing and expressing vulnerability. A 700-degree leader, therefore, is not only unable to grow but is often dangerous to the very people they are leading.

Re-read the story of the enthusiastic student in the blacksmith's shop who couldn't wait for the steel to get hot enough to forge (83). Trying to forge steel that is not hot enough is like to trying to lead without feeling vulnerable. This is the example of a 700-degree leader who is actually *more* dangerous to himself and to others than helpful as a leader.

> Standing in front of people who have expectations for leaders to be unfailing, never-disappointing, and always reassuring experts in the middle of a rapidly disorienting world, and

knowing that the truest thing we can say is, "I don't really know what to do next," is the moment when the leaders have to decide if they are going to go beyond 700 degrees.

And this is also, if we decide not to admit to the moment of vulnerability, when we are most dangerous to ourselves and others. We can tell ourselves that we are ready for this moment, that we know ourselves well and can "fake it until we make it." We can exude confidence that is beyond our competence and get others to follow close behind (even if they may get burned).[1] If being a grounded and teachable leader is critical for the tempered resilience needed to lead change, then the crucibles of leadership are challenges to our identity, and defending against those moments of vulnerability is what makes us dangerous. (*Tempered Resilience*, 84-85)

To engage the challenge of this kind of vulnerability, read the following section before engaging the reflection questions.

REFLECT

1. What has inspired you as you read this chapter of *Tempered Resilience*?

2. What raises questions that you would like to have clarified?

3. What do you find yourself resisting?

4. What changes are you considering in your own leadership because of reading this chapter?

Further Questions for Self-Reflection
Re-read this quote from Edwin Friedman:

[Leaders must have] a willingness to be exposed and vulnerable. One of the major limitations of imagination's fruits is the fear of standing out. It is more than a fear of criticism. It is anxiety at being alone, of being in a position where one

can rely little on others, a position that puts one's own resources to the test, a position where one will have to take
total responsibility for one's own response to the envi-
ronment. Leaders must not only not be afraid of that position; they must come to love it.[2]

■ When have you experienced this kind of vulnerability
of leadership? What happens internally when you feel
this way? What do you do at those moments?

■ Take one of the quotes about vulnerability in the book
and ask yourself:

♦ What is my history with vulnerable self-reflection?

♦ What messages have I learned about being vulnerable from my family of origin?

♦ What have I internalized about vulnerability as a
leader from my prior experiences?

♦ What does it feel like for *me* to find myself not as the
expert who has the answers but as the leader in need
of learning?

RELATE

■ With a trusted confidant or group, consider this quote
and the following conversation:

Self-reflection must lead to self-awareness, and self-
awareness—if courageous, honest, and practiced in a
place of engaged exposure—leads to feeling vulnerable.
(*Tempered Resilience*, 90)

■ Recall a time when you allowed yourself to function as
a 700-degree leader or were tempted to do so? What
did you do? What would you need to allow yourself to

DEVELOPING STRENGTH

Imagine yourself in this situation: you are leading a team of people, and your organization is in crisis. Maybe you are running out of money and people fear for their jobs. Maybe you lost a big donor or the attendance at church has been in a yearlong slide. Maybe it's a cultural or global phenomenon like the pandemic of 2020. You are sitting in a meeting and everybody is looking at you. And someone asks, "Well, what do *you* think we should do?"

You feel your face flush and your mouth go dry. Your mind is racing. You desperately want to convey confidence, and you want everyone to trust you. You are so tempted to put on a good face and fake it. And you fear that the next words you need to say are going to change everything.

You take a deep breath and say, "Friends. This is really a hard spot. And here is the honest answer: I don't know what to do."

How does that feel? If you are like me, even thinking about it makes you sick to your stomach. You can even picture the faces of your teammates staring at you in disbelief. You can hear, even in your mind, the muttering.

But if you can stand there and say that, experiencing the vulnerability of that moment, you can begin to develop the strength to lead your group into the transformation that comes in adaptive change. (*Tempered Resilience*, 80)

feel the vulnerability of self-reflection that would help you continue to develop resilience for leading?

- Discuss the bind described on page 98 that is often present for younger leaders, women, and leaders of color. There is real danger when people use leaders' honest vulnerability against them to denigrate or even remove them from leadership because of biases, but at the same time leaders can only grow by acknowledging their vulnerability, first to themselves and then, when it is safe, within the context of leadership challenges. How does that bind effect you and what can you do to create the contexts for the vulnerable self-reflection needed to continue to be forged into a tempered, resilient leader?

PRACTICE: PRAYER OF EXAMEN

At the end of the day, start with a prayer of gratitude for the day and call to mind the moments of your strongest feelings or experiences from the day. Pay attention to what you find yourself lingering on because they bring you comfort, mulling over as you replay them in your mind, or trying to push out of your mind because they are uncomfortable.

After calling to mind those moments, ask two questions:

1. Were those feelings *consolations*; that is, did they bring you closer to God? Did they help you grow in faith, hope, and love? Did they make you more generous and compassionate? Did they make you feel more alive, whole, and human? Did they lead you to feel more connected to others or inspire you to life-giving growth?

2. Were those feelings *desolations*; that is, did they lead you away from God, make you less faithful, hopeful, and loving? Did they cause you to become more self-centered or anxious? Did they lure you into doubt and confusion? Did they lead to the breakdown of relationships?[3]

In a journal, keep track of the insights from this daily prayer of examen. Trust that God is leading you toward your consolations and away from your desolations.

Ask yourself, What do I need to do *or* stop doing *to live into my consolations and leave behind my desolations?*

4

HOLDING

VULNERABLE LEADERSHIP REQUIRES
RELATIONAL SECURITY

The absurd expectation that a leader doesn't need
anyone else to lead well [is] one of the greatest
problems of the mental models of leadership.

T E M P E R E D   R E S I L I E N C E

READ chapter five of *Tempered Resilience.*

BECOMING A TEMPERED LEADER

Working: Leaders are formed in leading.

Heating: Strength is forged in self-reflection.

Holding: Vulnerable leadership requires relational security.

Hammering: Stress makes a leader.

Hewing: Resilience takes practice.

Tempering: Resilience comes through a rhythm of leading and not leading.

REVIEW

It may seem odd to compare the safety and security of relationships with something large, heavy, and inert like an anvil. Most of us don't think of an anvil as something that offers us comfort. But if we think of ourselves as heated, malleable, and even oozy during moments of vulnerability, then all of a sudden an anvil can be understood as a place of security—something that holds us safely when we are experiencing the heat of the crucible of leadership.

In this chapter we consider that a heavy, secure anvil is made up of numerous and diverse kinds of relationships. We need partners, teammates, colleagues, friends, family, and mentors. The more challenging the leadership task, the more heat we feel, the more exposed and vulnerable we are, the thicker the anvil will need to be.

Drawing on a concept first taught in the 1950s, we have learned a drama metaphor for the kinds of relationships that make up a heavy anvil. Leaders need trustworthy and skilled front-stage partners, coworkers, and teammates who share the leadership struggle with us. We also need backstage elders: supervisors, mentors, and coaches who help us lead even better when we step on to the front stage again. And we need offstage friends and family members who care even more about us than they do about our leadership work; people who give us the safety of love and acceptance that allows us to let go of our roles for a while and just be ourselves before we pick up the work again.

REFLECT

1. What has inspired you as you read this chapter of *Tempered Resilience*?

2. What raises questions that you would like to have clarified?

3. What do you find yourself resisting?

4. What changes are you considering in your own leadership because of reading this chapter?

Further Questions for Self-Reflection

- Duke Divinity School professor C. Kavin Rowe says, "We often think of resilience in individual terms: this or that person is resilient. But . . . start talking with resilient leaders and soon enough you will see that someone hoped for them in a time when they couldn't get back up. Resilience, in this understanding, is a communal practice, the fruit of a common life rooted in hope itself."[1] Who are the people in your life who "hoped for you" when you couldn't get back up?

- Read Exodus 18 and the brief comment on the passage from Jonathan Sacks on page 110 of *Tempered Resilience*. Who is the Jethro in your life? What would it mean for you to follow Jethro's advice in your own leadership?

- Read page 110 again and ask yourself: Who are the people who make up my anvil? Are there enough different people in the various stages in my life to truly hold me in my leadership vulnerability?

RELATE

- With a trusted confidant or group, consider this excerpt from my leadership experience:

  > In my own life and leadership, I have experienced that my worst times as a leader are not when things are going wrong but when I feel like I am facing the challenges and resistance alone. When my voice feels like it is echoing off of closed ears and hard hearts, when I think my best ideas are not being considered, that I am being marginalized by other organizational agendas or that the team stops functioning—for whatever reason—as a team.
  >
  > I have had those experiences when I was the most senior leader on the team and when I was a supporting cast member for another more senior leader. The hardest moments are not when we are facing a challenge but when the alliance—even momentarily—falls apart. (On the flip side, I was asked once in an interview what my greatest joy in leadership is. I knew immediately, "Having a big task—that might fail—that I get to take on with a great team." Big task. Some risk. Great team. That is joy.) (*Tempered Resilience*, 108)

- Make a list and discuss the depth and quality of the front stage (112), backstage (114), and offstage (118) relationships that make up your leadership anvil, and then take up this question from the reflection section, "Are there enough different people in the various stages in my life to truly hold me in my leadership vulnerability?"

PRACTICE

Re-read my experience of getting a cultural-humility coach (58). Then read "If I Were a Bishop."

THE ANVIL OF RELATIONSHIPS

A glance into the opening of the forge revealed an inferno of blazing fire and metal. The heatwaves created a gauzy view; the edges of the steel amid the fire blurred. In this state, now somewhere between 1,500 and 2,000 degrees, there were no exact lines between the edge of the steel and the fire that surrounded it. All was a bright, fiery glow.

"Okay, reach in with your tongs and pull out the steel. Notice the color." The glowing reds, yellows, oranges, and white pulsated the air.

"Put it immediately on the anvil. Don't wave it around. Don't carry it through the shop. Don't try to do anything to it until it is on the anvil. The only safe place for something that hot is on an anvil."

So, the moment of high heat, when the hammering process is going to begin, is when the shaping of the steel is most necessary—and most magical. But that magical moment is dependent on the most earthbound of items. That elixir-like molten steel is placed on a solid foundation. *Heating requires holding.*

In the same way that it is impossible to form raw steel without fire, it is impossible to shape that molten steel without an anvil. Indeed, it is dangerous to do so. Likewise in the formation of a tempered, resilient leader.

If the first critical element for a leader's development of resilience is vulnerable self-reflection, then the second, equally critical element is solid, safe relationships. Thick, heavy relationships. If vulnerable self-reflection that comes during a leadership challenge is like a fire, then relationships are like an anvil that can hold us in our most vulnerable, malleable, and oozy moments in life and leadership—and keep us and those around us safe. (*Tempered Resilience,* 104-5)

IF I WERE A BISHOP . . .

I once heard someone say that "hardship + relationship = resilience." While it is clear that the development of a tempered leader is indeed a bit more complex, this is a good, simple starting point for leaders who find themselves feeling the heat of leading and the intense 2,000-degree heat of vulnerability and self-awareness that comes from reflection.

Indeed, this is so critical to both developing the tempered resilience to lead change (and even just surviving the change process) that when I am asked what advice I would give to a change leader who is beginning to feel the heat of a change, I now have a standard response.

"If I were a bishop," I say half in jest while my bishop colleagues look on in bemusement, "and I could make a pronouncement that everyone would have to follow, I would want to issue a decree that to lead alone is reckless and arrogant; it is foolish and dangerous to both self and others. To lead alone usually results in either a failure of nerve or a failure of heart, which is to squander the valuable time, energy, and commitment of organizations and followers. And therefore, to lead a people without partners and mentors, full support of family and friends, and a lifetime commitment *at every moment that you are leading* of being in either psychological therapy, coaching, spiritual direction, or mentoring would be considered *leadership malpractice*."

This is why every doctoral student in my leading change cohort is required to do at least six months of therapy, spiritual direction, or engagement with an executive coach. This is why in my own life I have had years of executive coaching, spiritual direction, therapy, and more mentors than I can count.

When I talk to students who ask me how to find a mentor, I say, "Don't worry about finding a mentor. *Be a mentee*. Take responsibility for your life and your leadership, your growth and your formation. Let the work of leadership and the heat of self-reflection make you more self-aware and vulnerable to the place where you are feeling malleable and oozy, and humbly ask a wise person one question: 'Can I buy you a cup of coffee?' When they agree, as they usually will, then lay on the anvil and let them hold you with their advice and shape you with their questions."

Be a mentee. Show up oozy in your relationships and let them hold you when the hammering begins. (*Tempered Resilience*, 125)

Schedule a backstage conversation with a mentor, spiritual director, or coach about your leadership. Show up in a vulnerable and self-reflective place by reflecting on this question: Where do you think there are gaps in your capacity to lead change well? Be ready to discuss it with the person you are meeting with.

5

HAMMERING

STRESS MAKES A LEADER

Let the hammer do the work.

<small>BLACKSMITHING INSTRUCTOR</small>

READ chapter six of *Tempered Resilience.*

BECOMING A TEMPERED LEADER

Working: Leaders are formed in leading.

Heating: Strength is forged in self-reflection.

Holding: Vulnerable leadership requires relational security.

Hammering: Stress makes a leader.

Hewing: Resilience takes practice.

Tempering: Resilience comes through a rhythm of leading and not leading.

REVIEW

In this chapter we move from the heating and holding to the *hammering* process, from forging to *forming*. In the process of forming a leader with the capacity to face resistance with resilience, this is the place where reflection and relationships lead to a rule of life; that is, to spiritual and leadership practices that hammer in the most necessary characteristics. Using our blacksmithing analogy, hammering shapes the steel into the chisel that can bring about transformation of the rock into something of beauty. "In the same way, spiritual practices for a leader are not about being better at the practice itself but *forging the strength and character that has the resilience* to resist failure of nerve and overcome a failure of heart and hew stones of hope out of a mountain of despair" (132).

In this chapter we connect specific practices to the attributes that we need to develop in order to become tempered, resilient leaders. There is a deep dive into four very specific larger practices that give rise to specific disciplines for forming tempered resilience. See figure 5.1 for a diagram and description of these practices and attributes:

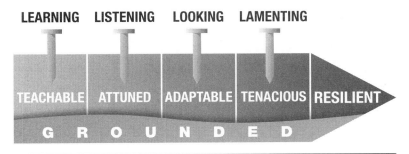

Figure 5.1

On pages 34–40 there is a description of each practice and a list of some disciplines for each practice. (For a fuller description see *Tempered Resilience*, 137). As you consider what you need to form tempered resilience in your life, consider how these disciplines and practices will help form you.

Which one or two disciplines from each practice could be a helpful part of your rule of life for resilient leadership?

Learning: Hammering in Humility

The best leaders are learners, and resilient leaders are most teachable. Leaders with a learning mindset (i.e., the belief that they *can* continue to grow) and a robust commitment to personal growth are often the most resilient leaders. Humility (or teachability) leads to greater capacity for standing up to resistance, because *there is an inherent assurance that this trial will—if nothing else—lead to my own growth.*

Some Disciplines for Practicing Learning

- A regular commitment to read, listen to podcasts, and take courses.
- Learn a new language.
- Join a conversation where people of widely divergent backgrounds and beliefs have a meal together and discuss issues for finding connection and common ground. Make your focus to truly understand a perspective that is different than the one you have.
- Travel to different cultures where you are not in the dominant majority.
- Take online courses in subjects that you neglected in your formal education.
- Learn a new hobby that requires you to master new abilities.
- Practice reverse mentoring in which a person who is younger or less experienced is the mentor, coach, or

teacher in a subject or skill that you didn't learn earlier in life. (I often joke that I could use an *eleven-year-old* coach to help me with all of my technology!)

Listening: Hammering in Attunement

The capacity to *attune* to both those inside and outside of their organization is a critical skill of change leaders. Attunement to our own people entails accompanying them through the process of change by helping *them* attune to those *for whom they are changing*. Developing resilience in a leader requires being able to listen to *both* the needs of the world and the fears of our people. It requires the capacity for navigating those competing values to *wisely* discern both the *strategies* of change and *pace* of change. This wisdom comes from a steadfast commitment to listen to God as much as we listen to our own people and to the pain of the world around us.

Some Disciplines for Practicing Listening

- Lectio divina. Lectio divina is a listening prayer that gives us space to hear the voice of God by repeatedly reading a simple passage of Scripture.[4]

- Communal reading of Scripture. The communal reading of Scripture involves listening to long passages of Scripture read audibly in a small group. While lectio divina is focused on short passages and longer silences, communal reading of Scripture emphasizes hearing the Word of God as a longer narrative.[5]

- Asking questions at a 2-1 ratio. I have a goal for every statement I make in a conversation or meeting to ask

FISHING WITH ZACH

(First, read the story about fishing with Zach on pages 129-30. Then, read the following analysis of what I learned from Zach.)

What I learned on that frustrating day and through Zach's clear, firm tutelage is an example of what has been termed *deliberate practice*. When the oft-quoted "10,000 hours" is cited as the path to mastery, what most forget is that it is ten thousand hours of *deliberate practice*.[1] It is ten thousand hours of *hard* work under the tutelage of an expert, focusing on the mistakes that need to be overcome, the undoing of bad habits, and the development of new skills. The key is that we sometimes have to sacrifice some of the enjoyment of the task to get better at the task. It isn't pleasant to sacrifice some of the joy of a good day fishing to get better at fishing. And the voice of the instructor, the strain to master a new task, the awkwardness of repetitively doing something that we are not already good at is hard, it is *stressful*.

It hammers away at us.

What is also often overlooked is that practice is something that we *do*, not something that we *think* about or even *pray* about. Deliberate practice is a kind of stress that we take on in our body so we can develop the poise to bring the strength and capacity formed by that stress to bear in a particular circumstance. . . .

While we remain committed to reflection and relationship, if we want to grow as resilient leaders we need to retrain our brains (which are part of our bodies!) through what we do with our hands, ears, eyes, and mouths. In the words of Dallas Willard, "A discipline is any activity within our power that we engage in to enable us to do what we cannot do by direct effort."[2]

To return to our blacksmith analogy, the hammers for shaping the raw material of a leader have *practical* but *indirect* purposes: Stress adds strength. Hammering shapes the steel into the chisel that can face the stone. In the same way, spiritual practices for a leader are not about being better at the practice itself but *forging the strength and character that has the resilience* to resist a failure of nerve and overcome a failure of heart and hew stones of hope out of a mountain of despair.

Spiritual practices for a leader are not about being better at the practice itself but forging the strength and character that has the resilience to resist a failure of nerve and overcome a failure of heart and hew stones of hope out of a mountain of despair.

Practices, then, are not about learning intellectual concepts but developing bodily capacity. *Practices create a kind of spiritual muscle memory, training us to respond to a crisis and resistance like it is second nature.* There is a huge difference between reading a book on the value of listening to a person and letting a conversation change your mind or give you empathy. There is a chasm of difference between hearing a sermon on forgiveness and being one of the parents forgiving the man who killed five schoolgirls in an Amish community or the members of the Emmanuel AME Church who *forgave* a white supremacist who shot their pastor and a group of congregants while in prayer for no other reason than because they were black.[3] Yes, we are shaped by our life experiences, our relationships, our beliefs, but so much of what creates the capacity to do repetitively the hard acts of leadership is shaped by previous actions that we have practiced numerous times. (*Tempered Resilience*, 130-33)

two questions I genuinely don't know the answer to. This is harder than it seems, but learning to ask good questions is one way to develop a greater capacity for listening and attuning to others.

▪ Make America Dinner Again. A nationwide organization founded in the wake of the 2016 election to address the growing political and ideological divide, they host "small dinners consist[ing] of respectful conversation, guided activities, and delicious food shared among 6-10 guests who have differing political viewpoints, and our country's best interests at heart." A great way to learn to listen to those that can be the hardest to hear.

Looking: Hammering in Adaptability

Most leaders have a necessary bias to action that urges them onward, but the resilient leader understands that gaining perspective, seeing the bigger picture, hearing the "music beneath the words" (the unspoken fears and anxieties, power plays, and disruptive movements that are fueling the systems' current functioning) is a critical practice for leading wise change. They need to be committed to first "see, not solve." Like a doctor searching for a diagnosis or a leader "on the balcony," looking is necessary for enduring. Resilient leaders must learn to pause and make as many observations and gather as many interpretations as possible before seeking to address challenges.

Some Disciplines for Practicing Looking

- Balcony journal. Writing a kind of after-action report of a conversation, leadership event, or conflict by writing about it three times in three different ways. The first time, write a first-person account that focuses on the feelings and experiences of being in the swirl of the dance floor. Then after setting it aside for a bit, return and rewrite it from the third person as if you are watching yourself from the balcony. Then after letting it sit again, write a coaching note to yourself about the next steps for leading through that circumstance.

- Balcony conversation. Whenever you have a leadership experience that created a feeling of being overwhelmed by the energy on the dance floor, ask a trusted coach or mentor to have a balcony conversation to help you gain perspective and to see some of the larger systems or patterns of behavior that triggered your feelings.

Lamenting: Hammering in Tenacity

Adaptive change entails helping people navigate the losses that come with change, requires learning, and results in loss. Indeed, the reality of loss and the desire to avoid that loss triggers the most significant resistance in both leaders and the people they lead.

How do leaders develop the tenacity to endure loss? Through the spiritual practice of lament. Laments invite God into the swirl of loss and remind us that our capacity to lead in the world, especially when leading at the place of despair, resistance, and the failures of nerve and heart, is met with the power of the God who is present and is active.

Some Disciplines for Practicing Lament

- "Get proximate to people who are suffering." These words of justice advocate Bryan Stevenson in his 2018 commencement address at Bates College challenge us to fight against our tendency to distance and deny the pain of the world, by intentionally moving closer to people who are experiencing lament-worthy conditions.[6]
- Regularly read the Psalms of Lament.

- Use the pattern of a lament to write a lament of your own, putting the pain of the people you are trying to serve and the people you are leading and their concerns into the texts.

- If you are a pastor, add prayers of lament regularly into your worship service.

- Practice the discipline of learning to "see, not solve" a problem. Particularly when confronting the brutal facts of the pain points of the people around you—and don't do anything yet. See (not solve), lament first, and let those laments have their work in you.

REFLECT

1. What has inspired you as you read this chapter of *Tempered Resilience*?

2. What raises questions that you would like to have clarified?

3. What do you find yourself resisting?

4. What changes are you considering in your own leadership because of reading this chapter?

Further Questions for Self-Reflection

Read Dr. King's rule for the nonviolent civil rights movement on page 135 of *Tempered Resilience*. Then consider the following questions.

- Which of these practices, disciplines, or rules are specific to the goals of Dr. King's movement?

- Why do you think he picked these?

- What is the formative goal of these practices?

- If tempered resilience is the formative goal of your spiritual practices, how might you need to adapt them?

RELATE

With a trusted confidant or group discuss the following questions.

- What are the practices in your rule of life that you have used consciously or unconsciously up to this point in your life?
- How have they changed over the years and why?
- Discuss the following self-reflection question: If tempered resilience is the formative goal of your spiritual practices, how might you need to adapt them?

PRACTICE: RULE OF LIFE FOR RESILIENT LEADERS

RULE OF LEADERSHIP

A rule, therefore, is adapted to the *mission* of the group or the individual disciple. While many different practices (and disciplines) show up in spiritual formation literature, there is an overlap with leadership-development activities and exercises that, even without the religious or theological commitment, are helpful for a leader. In our case the capacity to lead change in the face of resistance requires a set of practices that a leader would take on. In other words, most rules are for a *way of living* as a Christian, but I am suggesting a rule for a *way of leading* and even more specifically for answering the question: *What practices of a rule of life form leadership resilience for facing resistance? (Tempered Resilience*, 135)

Create a rule of life based on the following template, which uses the four practices that hammer in the qualities needed for resilience.

RULE OF LIFE

What characteristics do I most need to develop in my life to be a tempered, resilient leader (grounded identity, teachable, attuned, adaptable, tenacious)?

Which larger practices or specific disciplines do I need as part of a rule of life to develop those qualities?

Daily Practices or Disciplines:

1.

2.

Weekly Practices or Disciplines:

1.

2.

Monthly Practices or Disciplines:

1.

2.

Quarterly or Annual Practices or Disciplines:

1.

2.

6

HEWING

RESILIENCE TAKES PRACTICE

Leadership should generate capacity, not dependency.

Ronald Heifetz

READ chapter seven of *Tempered Resilience.*

BECOMING A TEMPERED LEADER

Working: Leaders are formed in leading.

Heating: Strength is forged in self-reflection.

Holding: Vulnerable leadership requires relational security.

Hammering: Stress makes a leader.

Hewing: Resilience takes practice.

Tempering: Resilience comes through a rhythm of leading and not leading.

REVIEW

In a forward to a Jewish commentary on the first five books of the Bible, Ronald Heifetz writes,

> In biblical terms, we might ask how a culture of dependency
> can transform into a culture of widely distributed leadership,

how a people enslaved for generations can become a society in which all members are called upon to take responsibility whenever they see fit, whoever they are.[1]

This chapter examines how the formation of a change leader forms people who do in fact change.

The hewing practice involves the following practices (see fig. 6.1).

Managing reactivity. Managing reactivity is the way leaders keep their emotions under control well enough to calmly and wisely make the best decision for furthering the transformational process that leads to the organization's missional objectives. In managing reactivity, a tempered, resilient leader is able to bring wise *responses* in the face of resistance rather than unreflective and emotion-laden *reactions* (see *Tempered Resilience*, 165).

Reframing. Reframing is the capacity of a leader to create a vision for change for an organization or community that is consistent with their sense of shared identity, history, and values, while adapting to the present challenges in a way that allows them to thrive and fulfill their mission. "In an adaptive change process, vision is usually not about a *new* vision but a *renewed* vision. It is helping people see what they have missed and recover their best intentions and dreams that have become set aside or discarded and then adapted to a new day" (see *Tempered Resilience*, 173).

Reorienting. Reorienting requires waypoint-to-waypoint navigating toward the vision of change that requires making strategic decisions, testing, learning, and adjusting. Reorienting is "pivoting." A pivot is a "change of strategy without

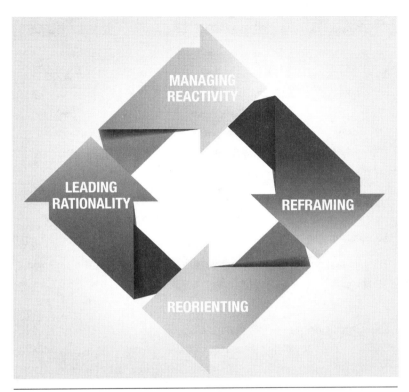

Figure 6.1

a change of vision" and keeps the change process moving forward. "To reorient requires that we move *forward* in a concrete way. Moving forward means that we have to make some decisions. Every time we learn, adjust, and decide on a next step to the next waypoint, we build momentum for change. And momentum and the feelings of hope it inspires increase resilience" (see *Tempered Resilience*, 180).

Leading relationally. Leading relationally utilizes emotional intelligence and empathy to stay connected to the people who are most resistant to the change process *and* to support those allies who are most committed to partnering with the leader

FORMING RESILIENT PEOPLE

We move from the process of forging steel into a tool that has the strength to hew hope from despair to using that very tool (ourselves!) to shape the resilience and adaptive capacity of our congregations, organizations, and institutions. If "you are your only tool," then how do you put yourself to work shaping your people? If leadership is about generating capacity and not dependency, then how can we lead in such a way that grows the capacity of our people?[2]

How do we shape the very people who are often themselves part of the resistant, sabotaging core, into a people who can grow and face their biggest challenges and thrive?[3]

The ultimate goal of adaptive change is not to master a pain-free solution to a pressing problem, it's to create adaptive capacity: the wisdom, courage, and resilience within a people to learn and survive losses. . . .

If resilient leadership is about taking responsibility to face often brutal reality with hope, to find meaning in setbacks, to use creative adaptations to work through challenges, and to overcome both a failure of nerve that will shrink back and a failure of heart that devolves into cynicism, how do resilient leaders form a resilient people? *The same principles apply.*

- A group is formed for bringing change because of *challenges* facing the organization.

- The group needs to develop and reaffirm a clear, *grounded*, organizational identity and mission, and grow in the capacity to be *teachable, attuned, adaptable, and tenacious.*

- The group needs to be able to practice vulnerable *reflection* and experience the trust and safety of strong, supportive *relationships.*

- The group needs to be led through the change by a resilient leader who regularly practices and demonstrates the value of *learning, listening, looking, and lamenting.*

But a set of leadership *skills* are also needed for leading change. These are the skills for the *practice of tempered change leadership*, and when exercised wisely and well they not only increase the odds for bringing change but form a more resilient people to face those odds, whatever they may be. (*Tempered Resilience*, 163-64)

in the transformation necessary for the organization. "This skill set doesn't come easy to most visionary leaders. We tend to lead by planning, enthusiasm, voice, and inspiring ideas instead of through the patient cultivating of relationships. But by learning to listen more, ask lots of questions, and develop deeper empathy with those who are feeling the loss of change, we will find that people—over time—will trust us enough to keep moving with us into the changes we need to make" (see *Tempered Resilience*, 185).

REFLECT

1. What has inspired you as you read this chapter of *Tempered Resilience*?

2. What raises questions that you would like to have clarified?

3. What do you find yourself resisting?

4. What changes are you considering in your own leadership because of reading this chapter?

Further Questions for Self-Reflection

- In what ways do your leadership practices create capacity rather than dependency in your team or community?

- Have you experienced the challenges of being a second-chair leader who needs to *lead up* to a supervisor that may be growing weary with the change process? If so, explain.

- Read the section on page 188 of *Tempered Resilience* on how peacemongers increase sabotage and resistance in an organization. In what ways have you been a peace monger or been the creative leader who experienced sabotage because a senior leader was a peacemonger?

RELATE

With a trusted confidant or group, discuss the self-reflection question, "In what ways do your leadership practices create capacity rather than dependency in your team or community?" If these are people who have worked with you or observed your leadership, ask them to give their perspective on your leadership practices.

PRACTICE

The key point of this chapter on hewing is *resilience takes practice.* A trusted means for practicing leadership is through after-action case studies.

For example, throughout *Tempered Resilience* I reflect on a story of sabotage that occurred during a capital campaign and nine-year building project while I was a pastor. I use it as a case study to evaluate my own process of leading change and developing the adaptive capacity of the San Clemente congregation.

In a similar way, write and reflect on a case study from an organization you either led or observed and look for the ways that you or the other leaders engaged the four leadership

skills in the transformation process: managing reactivity, reframing, reorienting, and leading relationally.

*In what ways did you or the leaders you observed demon-
strate tempered resilience well in using those four leadership
practices, and in what ways could the leadership response have
been stronger?*

*What will you do or not do the next time you use a change
process to engage those tempered-resilience leadership practices?*

*Is there something you could add to your rule of life for a re-
silient leader that will help you grow in these leadership practices?*

7

TEMPERING

*RESILIENCE COMES THROUGH A RHYTHM OF LEADING
AND NOT LEADING*

> *Resilience comes from stress that creates strength. At
> the same time, too much stress means that both steel
> and leaders become brittle instruments that crumble
> beneath the task. This is the delicate balance.*
>
> TEMPERED RESILIENCE

READ chapter eight of *Tempered Resilience.*

BECOMING A TEMPERED LEADER

Working: Leaders are formed in leading.

Heating: Strength is forged in self-reflection.

Holding: Vulnerable leadership requires relational security.

Hammering: Stress makes a leader.

Hewing: Resilience takes practice.

Tempering: Resilience comes through a rhythm of leading and not leading.

REVIEW

Perhaps the lesson most often overlooked by change leaders is that tempered resilience requires a rhythm of leading *and* not leading. Indeed, the critical element that brings the flexibility and durability of a *tempered* tool requires that the process for making the tool includes times of *slow* cooling and the release of stress. This is not just a cry for the self-care of leaders (though that is very important), but is also an intentional strategy of *both taking on and letting go the demands of leadership in order to be transformed* into a tempered, resilient leader.

THE RHYTHM OF STRESS AND REST

If the leader's failure of nerve can be attributed to being too soft and too compliant with the anxiety of the system, failure of heart is the outcome of a leader that has become discouraged, emotionally disconnected, and too brittle. A *rhythm* of stress and rest tempers a tool and builds in the strength and flexibility that bring resilience. As two researchers concluded, "The key to resilience is trying really hard, then stopping, recovering, and then trying again."[1]

Tempering, again, is not a one-time plunge into a cold pool or a once-a-year vacation or retreat. It is a regular, repetitive process: The heat of the crucible of leadership is only intensified through reflection. The hammering of spiritual practices is only intensified through the practice of leadership. Both shaping the leader into a tool and the use of the tool is intense and hammers in stress in the leader. But, in both shaping and leading, the actual *tempering* occurs during times of cooling or quenching, slowly releasing leadership responsibilities at least temporarily.

This rhythm is the process for a tempered leader (see. fig. 7.1): *heating* through work and reflection, *holding* of good relationships both personally and professionally, the *hammering* of spiritual practices and the practice of leadership, and the *tempering* that comes through cooling periods of rest and release from leading, and then repeated. (*Tempered Resilience*, 196-97)

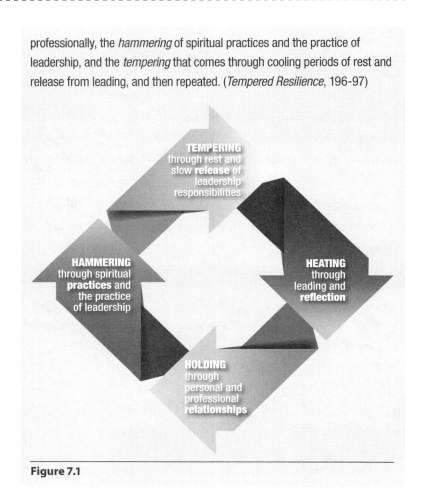

Figure 7.1

REFLECT

1. What has inspired you as you read this chapter of *Tempered Resilience*?

2. What raises questions that you would like to have clarified?

3. What do you find yourself resisting?

4. What changes are you considering in your own leadership because of reading this chapter?

A Further Question for Self-Reflection

■ Reflect on the following: "This rhythm of working and not working, leading and not leading, toiling and enjoying, being diligent and being thankful, of good ministry and good life creates both a resilient leader and a healthy community" (203). To what degree does your own life and leadership reflect this rhythm?

RELATE

With a trusted confidant or group discuss the following passage.

A TEMPERED LEADER

Hewing hope from despair is hard work. It's not something that just happens. Transforming discord into a beautiful symphony takes deliberate, diligent, and dedicated people. Leading adaptive change requires more from us than we can muster with our good intentions. It requires forging.

A tempered leader is formed in the crucible of leading through reflection, relationships, and a rule of life in a rhythm of leading and not leading.

A tempered leader has resilience formed through a grounded identity, and teachable, attuned, adaptable, and tenacious character.

A tempered leader hammers resilience into people through managing reactivity, reframing, reorienting, and leading relationally.

And like a tempered tool that has been made stronger and more flexible than the raw material alone, the leader often needs to be sharpened, honed, and reforged again and again. And again. (*Tempered Resilience*, 207)

What restorative acts are part of your life? Are they valuable enough to make them a regular rhythm of your leadership? What would you have to change about the rhythm of your life to include these restorative activities?

PRACTICE

What do you need to add to your rule of life that will enable you to have a regular rhythm of *not* leading?

8

THE WHY OF LEADERSHIP

Why should anyone work so hard to
face such resistance for so long?

A Leadership Coach

READ *Tempered Resilience*'s epilogue.

REVIEW

A final word and then a final lesson.

In the work our team at Fuller Seminary developed on *vocation formation*, we came up with a concept we called the "central integration question" (CIQ). The answer to the CIQ would give shape to our vocation and reason for engaging in the learning, the formation, the work, and even the potential suffering that came from responding to the voice of God's Spirit. The question is, At this point of your Christian journey, how do you envision your calling to God's mission in the world?

We believe that our ability to articulate a clear, compelling answer to that question throughout our lives serves as both the waypoint for a formative journey and offers the motivation for continuing as a leader in the face of external challenges and internal resistance.

My long-time answer to the CIQ is *to form Christian leaders for a changing world*. And as important as it is to articulate that answer, even more important is the *why* behind it.

In this final chapter we consider the emotional cost of leading change and the toll it takes on the leader. We are reminded that (1) "most change initiatives fail" (214) and (2) "adaptive change only occurs when the work is 'given back to the people'" (215). So, in this final session of this study guide we consider the *compelling why* needed to endure resistance when leading change.

TO LOVE GOD AND LOVE OTHERS

Leadership is born not of the desire to lead but—at the center of our being—out of *a call to service in light of the brutal facts of the world.* It flows not from a desire to achieve, succeed, or accomplish, but to *serve* at the point of real need and experiencing that need as one's own calling.[1]

Leadership expert Marty Linsky says in an interview with *Faith and Leadership*, "People who are willing to take the risks of exercising leadership do so *on behalf of something they care deeply about.*"[2] In other words, there must be a compelling *why* for leading that is about a genuine need in the world.

Christian leadership that flows from the center of our being must begin in aligning our motivations with the purposes of God; the intentions and activities we see in the Scriptures come from the center of *Jesus'* being—the things God deeply cares about (John 1:18). In his book *The Jesus Creed*, New Testament scholar Scot McKnight writes about Jesus' most audacious and innovative mash-up of the commands of God. These two lines, writes McKnight, are the starting point for any spiritual formation and the key to understanding the unique adaptation that Jesus' presence brings to the revelation of God given to Israel.[3] For McKnight, Jesus' teaching leads to the "first amendment" to the fundamental commandment given to God's people. And it was both a scandal and an act of leadership that demands our attention if we too are going to lead others into the mission of God in the world. . . .

The end or goal of life for Jesus—whether for an individual or a community— is to love God *and* love others. *And they are equal in importance.* You cannot have one without the other. You must, must, must have both. Jesus says that to live with the ultimate end in mind, to live out the greatest commandment, to live in a way that pleases God is *not just to love God but also to love the world the way God so loves it.*[4]

It is this conviction that forms the *why* of leadership. For followers of Jesus there is nothing we are called to care about as much as the love and justice of God reaching our neighbor and being expressed in all of creation. In theological terms, the venture capitalist I made my innovation pitch to in Silicon Valley was challenging the seminary professor about the most basic question asked of Jesus: "Who is my neighbor?" (*Tempered Resilience*, 211-14)

REFLECT

1. What has inspired you as you read this chapter of *Tempered Resilience*?

2. What raises questions that you would like to have clarified?

3. What do you find yourself resisting?

4. What changes are you considering in your own leadership because of reading this chapter?

Further Questions for Self-Reflection

■ How do you respond to the idea that the love of neighbor is the compelling reason for churches and

Christian organizations to undergo deep, transformative change?

- What are your initial responses to the following selection from *Tempered Resilience*?

> Success or failure in leading change is as much about what happens in the lives of the people as what happens in the organization. The long-term fruitfulness is people who grow in their adaptive capacity to become lifelong learners who learn to navigate necessary losses with hope and courage. These leaders, formed to be used by God, will also encourage genuine transformation wherever they go. The development of people with the capacity to hew hope out of despair and transform discord into harmonious communities— wherever they are—is more important than any one change effort. (215)

RELATE

With a trusted confidant or group discuss these questions: What is your personal, compelling *why* for leadership? Why do you work so hard to bring change?

PRACTICE

Write your compelling *why* in a short, easily memorized phrase. Aim to make it less than ten words. Paste that compelling *why* in a place where you can see it often and allow it to continue to bring you back to the focus needed to lead change.

And as someone who—by even reading *Tempered Resilience* and working through this study guide—is helping me live out my calling to "form Christian leaders for a changing world," know that I bless you and offer my prayers for you and your leadership.

May God bless you as you lead. Because of your leadership, may your congregation, your organization, your family, and community become—even a bit more—the answer to Jesus' prayer to his Father in heaven, "Your kingdom come. Your will be done, on earth as it is in heaven" (Matthew 6:10).

NOTES

INTRODUCTION
[1]David Brooks, "Students Learn from People They Love," *New York Times*, January 17, 2019, www.nytimes.com/2019/01/17/opinion/learning-emotion-education.html.

1 HEWING HOPE AND THE MOUNTAIN OF DESPAIR
[1]"Rather than standing out from others (differentiation), a person may stand outside of their circle (cutoff). Genuine separateness is differentiation within a relationship, not independence of it. Cutoff is an exaggeration of the need to be separate—'I can only count on myself' or 'I'll do it alone.' Again, the difference between people who cut off and those who take strong positions is in their functioning. Cutoff is reactive. It's an automatic defense." Peter L. Steinke, *Congregational Leadership in Anxious Times: Being Calm and Courageous No Matter What* (Lanham, MD: Rowman & Littlefield, 2006), 27.
[2]"In the moment of crisis, you will not rise to the occasion; you will default to your training." Tod Bolsinger, *Canoeing the Mountains: Christian Leadership in Uncharted Territory*, exp. ed. (Downers Grove, IL: InterVarsity Press, 2015), 32.

2 WORKING: LEADERS ARE FORMED IN LEADING
[1]Abigail Adams, cited in Doris Kearns Goodwin, *Leadership: In Turbulent Times* (New York: Simon & Schuster, 2018), loc. 80, Kindle.

3 HEATING: STRENGTH IS FORGED IN SELF-REFLECTION
[1]Tomas Chamorro-Premuzic, "Why Do So Many Incompetent Men Become Leaders?" *Harvard Business Review*, August 22, 2013, https://hbr.org/2013/08/why-do-so-many-in competent-men.
[2]Edwin H. Friedman, *A Failure of Nerve: Leadership in the Age of the Quick Fix* (New York: Church Publishing, 2017), loc. 3338, Kindle.
[3]Kevin O'Brien, *The Ignatian Adventure: Experiencing the Spiritual Exercises of St. Ignatius in Daily Life* (Chicago: Loyola Press, 2011), 78.

4 HOLDING: VULNERABLE LEADERSHIP
REQUIRES RELATIONAL SECURITY
[1]C. Kavin Rowe, "Cultivating Resilience in Christ-Shaped Leaders," *Faith and Leadership*, April 23, 2012, https://faithandleadership.com/c-kavin-rowe-cultivating-resilience -christ-shaped-leaders.

5 HAMMERING: STRESS MAKES A LEADER
[1]"As defined, deliberate practice is a very specialized form of practice. You need a teacher or coach who assigns practice techniques designed to help you improve on very specific skills. That teacher or coach must draw from a highly developed body of knowledge about the best way to teach these skills." Anders Ericsson, *Peak: Secrets from the New Science of Expertise* (New York: Houghton Mifflin Harcourt, 2016), 100. See also Angela Duckworth, *Grit: The Power of Passion and Perseverance* (New York: Simon & Schuster, 2018), chap. 7; and Angela Duckworth, "Duckworth: 'Deliberate Practice' Is an Important Element of Grit," *Education Dive*, April 18, 2018, www.educationdive.com/news/duckworth -deliberate-practice-is-an-important-element-of-grit/521559.

---

[2]Dallas Willard, *The Divine Conspiracy: Rediscovering Our Hidden Life in God* (New York: HarperCollins, 2014), 353.

[3]See Donald B. Kraybill, Steven M. Nolt, and David L. Weaver-Zercher, *Amish Grace* (San Francisco: John Wiley, 2007). Cf. Mark Berman, "'I Forgive You.' Relatives of Charleston Church Shooting Victims Address Dylann Roof," *Washington Post*, June 19, 2015, www.washingtonpost.com/news/post-nation/wp/2015/06/19/i-forgive-you-relatives-of-charleston-church-victims-address-dylann-roof.

[4]My favorite way of practicing lectio divina is through the British Jesuits' website *Pray as You Go*, https://pray-as-you-go.org.

[5]Fuller Seminary has developed a website to make the communal reading of Scripture accessible and easy for any group. See "Communal Reading of Scripture," *Fuller Studio*, https://fullerstudio.fuller.edu/series/communal-reading-scripture.

[6]Doug Hubley, "'Get Proximate to People Who Are Suffering,' Bryan Stevenson Tells Bates Commencement Audience," *Bates College News*, May 27, 2018, www.bates.edu/news/2018/05/27/get-proximate-to-people-who-are-suffering-bryan-stevenson-tells-bates-college-commencement-audience.

6 HEWING: RESILIENCE TAKES PRACTICE

[1]Ronald Heifetz, in the foreword to Jonathan Sacks, *Lessons in Leadership: A Weekly Reading of the Jewish Bible* (New York: Toby Press, 2015), loc. 181, Kindle.

[2]Ronald Heifetz, foreword to Jonathan Sacks, *Lessons in Leadership: A Weekly Reading of the Jewish Bible* (New York: Toby Press, 2015), loc. 178, Kindle.

[3]"Adaptive leadership is the practice of mobilizing people to tackle tough challenges and thrive." Ronald A. Heifetz, Marty Linsky, and Alexander Grashow, *The Practice of Adaptive Leadership: Tools and Tactics for Changing Your Organization and the World* (Cambridge, MA: Harvard Business School, 2009), loc. 383, Kindle.

7 TEMPERING: RESILIENCE COMES THROUGH A RHYTHM OF LEADING AND NOT LEADING

[1]Shawn Achor and Michelle Gielan, "Resilience Is About How You Recharge, Not How You Endure," *Harvard Business Review*, June 24, 2016, https://hbr.org/2016/06/resilience-is-about-how-you-recharge-not-how-you-endure.

8 THE WHY OF LEADERSHIP

[1]Jim Collins discusses his view that real change starts not in a vision but in a deep look at the brutal facts of a situation. Jim Collins, "Keeping the Flywheel in Motion," *Knowledge Project Podcast*, accessed October 8, 2019, https://fs.blog/jim-collins.

[2]Marty Linsky, "Martin Linsky: Pushing Against the Wind," *Faith & Leadership*, September 27, 2010, www.faithandleadership.com/marty-linsky-pushing-against-wind; emphasis added.

[3]"The first principle of spiritual formation is this: A spiritually formed person loves God and others." Scot McKnight, *Jesus Creed: Loving God, Loving Others* (London: Paraclete Press, 2004), 3.

[4]Tod Bolsinger, "The Jesus Creed: Love God, Love Neighbors," *Tod Bolsinger* (blog), May 9, 2007, http://bolsinger.blogs.com/weblog/2007/05/the_jesus_creed.html.

ALSO BY
TOD BOLSINGER

TOD BOLSINGER
AUTHOR OF *CANOEING THE MOUNTAINS*

TEMPERED
RESILIENCE

HOW LEADERS ARE
FORMED IN THE
CRUCIBLE OF
CHANGE

TOD BOLSINGER

CANOEING
THE
MOUNTAINS

CHRISTIAN
LEADERSHIP IN
UNCHARTED TERRITORY